George Mason Library
2601 Cameron Mills Rd.
Alexandria, Virginia 22302

D1300658

Kings and Queens of West Africa

Sylviane Anna Diouf

Franklin Watts
A Division of Grolier Publishing
New York • London • Hong Kong • Sydney
Danbury, Connecticut

Note to readers: Definitions for words in **bold** can be found in the Glossary at the back of this book.

Cover illustration by Gary Overacre

Photographs ©: AP/Wide World Photos: 3 top, 33 (Jean-Marc Bouju), 22 (Kamran Jebreili); Art Resource, NY: 29, 31 (The Newark Art Museum), 35 (Aldo Tutino), 26, 30, 37 (Werner Forman Archive Wallace Collection, London); Bridgeman Art Library International Ltd., London/New York: 15 (HSC104230/Horse and Rider. Djenne, Mali. Terracotta, 44 x 17 x 30 cm. Private Collection/Heini Schneebeli), 36 (HSC104296/Goldweight representing two crocodiles with a shared stomach. Asante, Ghana.18th -19th century. Brass. Private Collection/Heini Schneebeli); Christie's Images: 39; Corbis Sygma: 14 (Thierry Prat); Corbis-Bettmann: 16 (Paul Almasy), 20 top (Christel Gerstenberg), 24 (Wolfgang Käehler), 17 (Charles & Josette Lenars), 48; Courtesy of the Author: 44 top; Liaison Agency, Inc.: 25 (Wolfgang Käehler), 44 bottom (Zillioux); Mary Evans Picture Library: 47 (Le Journal Illustre), 18, 21, 28, 34, 42; Photo Researchers: 40 (George Holton), 50 (Carl Purcell); Reprinted from "Esquisses Senegalaises: 43, 45 (Original Illustrations by Abbe David Boilat); Stock Montage, Inc.: 8, 9, 19, 23; The Art Archive: 12; Victor Englebert: 3 bottom, 6, 11, 20 bottom, 32, 38, 46, 52; Woodfin Camp & Associates: 53 (M. & E. Bernheim).

Maps by XNR Productions.

Visit Franklin Watts on the Internet at:
http://publishing.grolier.com

Library of Congress Cataloging-in-Publication Data

Diouf, Sylviane Anna
    Kings and queens of West Africa / by Sylviane Anna Diouf
        p.   cm.— (Watts Library)
    Includes bibliographical references and index.
    Summary: A survey of the historical regions and kingdoms of West Africa including biographies of Mansa Musa, Emporer of Mali (c. 1280–1337); Osei Tutu, King of Asante (c. 1660–1717); and Ndate Yalla Mbodj, Queen of Walo (c. 1810–1860).
    ISBN 0-531-20375-1 (lib. bdg.)   0-531-16536-1 (pbk.)
    1. Africa, West—Kings and rulers—Biography—Juvenile literature. 2. Africa, West—History—Juvenile literature. [I. Kings, queens, rulers, etc. 2. Africa, West—History.] I. Title. II. Series.
DT475.5 .K35 2000
966'.02'0922—dc21   99-086209
[B]

GROLIER
PUBLISHING

©2000 by Sylviane Anna Diouf
All rights reserved. Published simultaneously in Canada.
Printed in the United States of America.
1 2 3 4 5 6 7 8 9 10 R 09 08 07 06 05 04 03 02 01 00

Contents

Chapter One
Kings and Queens of Africa 5

Chapter Two
**The Kingdoms and
Empires of West Africa** 9

Chapter Three
Mansa Musa, Emperor of Mali 13

Chapter Four
Osei Tutu, King of Asante 27

Chapter Five
Ndate Yalla Mbodj, Queen of Walo 41

Chapter Six
West Africa Today 51

54 **Glossary**

56 **To Find Out More**

60 **A Note on Sources**

61 **Index**

Rabat

MOROCCO

WESTERN
SAHARA

S A H A R A

Nouakchott

MAURITANIA

M A L I

MALI

NIGER

Dakar

SENEGAL

Banjul

THE GAMBIA

Bamako

Niger R.

BURKINA
FASO

Niamey

Bissau

GUINEA-BISSAU

GUINEA

Ouagadougou

Lake Chad

Conakry

SIERRA
LEONE

CÔTE
D'IVOIRE
(IVORY
COAST)

GHANA

TOGO

BENIN

NIGERIA

Abuja

Freetown

Monrovia

LIBERIA

Accra

Niger R.

CAMEROON

Abidjan

Lomé

Porto-
Novo

EQUATORIAL
GUINEA

Atlantic
Ocean

GABON

	The Empire of Mali
	The Asante Kingdom
	The Kingdom of Walo
	Modern national boundary
⊛	Modern capital city

AFRICA

Area
enlarged

Indian
Ocean

Atlantic
Ocean

N

0   500 mi.

0   500 km

Chapter One

Kings and Queens of Africa

Africa is a continent of great natural diversity—burning deserts, snowy mountains, lush forests, dry savannas, and majestic rivers. Africa's 800 million people are as diverse as its landscape. Thousands of different populations live in the continent's fifty-three countries. Africans speak 25 percent of the 6,000 languages that exist on Earth.

For tens of thousands of years, Africans have shared the beauty of this vast continent. The peoples used Africa's immense resources while each population developed its own culture, language, and traditions. This amazing diversity could be a source of richness or of division, but from the earliest times Africa has had great leaders who united diverse communities into strong nations.

The kings and queens of Africa were concerned not only with power and the expansion of their kingdoms, but also with justice, education, arts, crafts, agriculture, and trade.

Some ruled in difficult times. The arrival of the Europeans, the rise of the slave trade, and colonization unsettled their territories and the continent as a whole. Rulers faced external threats and internal divisions, and they had to invent ways to govern and protect their communities.

Ghana, in West Africa, has beautiful forests.

Accounts of the kings and queens of Africa have been passed from one generation to the next through stories and songs. Starting in the eighth century, travelers from North Africa recorded their observations of African rulers in books and letters. Africans, writing in Arabic, did the same, starting in the 1500s. Europeans first arrived in Africa in 1444, and they left records of the rulers and the courts they visited. Natives and foreigners have helped us know the rulers who, with their people, have created the history of Africa.

For the series, *Kings and Queens of Africa*, the continent has been divided into four parts: West, Central, Southern, and East. Each area has characteristics that helped shape the cultures that developed there. West Africa was a crossroads for trade, and kingdoms and empires based largely on commerce rose in the region. East Africa was molded by the great variety of its peoples. Central Africa was transformed by the migration of the Bantu population from the northwest. Large movements of population changed the course of Southern Africa's history.

Each book in this series looks at different eras to show how the region evolved through time and the most significant rulers of the region. Some were more famous than others, and some well-known figures do not appear here. I have presented social, political, and cultural innovators who connected their kingdoms to a much larger world, defended their territory against foreign invasions, or brought various groups together into one people. These rulers left important legacies.

A nineteenth-century view of the city of Timbuktu, in Mali, West Africa

Chapter Two

The Kingdoms and Empires of West Africa

For many centuries there have been organized states and powerful empires in West Africa. Their wealth came from agriculture and mining, which gave rise to trade through the region and with Central and North Africa. The kingdoms and empires in the area expanded to control the trade activity.

The stories of three rulers convey the history of the region and show the important role trade played. Mansa Musa (c. 1280–1337), emperor of Mali, established trade and cultural relations with the Islamic world. Osei Tutu (c. 1660–1717) of Asante (Ghana) used commercial ties with the Europeans to expand his territories. Queen Ndate Yalla Mbodj (c. 1810–1860) of Walo (in Senegal) tried to protect the trade and independence of her kingdom from a French takeover.

A Powerful Muslim State

Ancient Ghana was the first important empire to rise in West Africa. It dominated the region in the eighth century, but later weakened. Ancient Mali was the second important West African empire. In 1235, its founder, Sundiata Keita, and his army conquered the crumbling Ghana Empire.

By the mid-eleventh century, the rulers, many of the educated people, and the traders had become **Muslims**. They were followers of **Islam,** the religion brought by the Prophet **Muhammad**. The empire of Mali opened trade and cultural relations with other Muslim countries, such as Morocco, Egypt, and Arabia. Mali reached its height under Emperor Mansa Musa in the fourteenth century. It was one of the best organized and largest empires in the world at that time.

Europeans and the Slave Trade

In the forest regions of southern West Africa, large kingdoms arose in the fourteenth century. Shortly after, Europeans arrived and built forts on the Atlantic Coast, many of them on the Gold Coast (present-day Ghana), to control the gold and slave trades. The Europeans provided weapons to local rulers, who fought each other to expand their territories. They sold prisoners of war to the European merchants. The prisoners were then shipped to the Americas as slaves. In the seventeenth century, the kingdom of Asante, led by Osei Tutu, became the most powerful state in the region.

The Beginning of Colonization

The nineteenth century was a time of great changes. The slave trade and slavery were abolished by 1848, and the people could live in peace after 300 years of devastation. But it also saw the end of a world: The last African kingdoms disappeared as the colonial powers—France, Great Britain, and Portugal—took control. The first kingdom to be conquered by the French was Walo, in Senegal, ruled by Queen Ndate Yalla Mbodj. By the end of the century, West Africa was totally conquered.

Much of the West African landscape is lowland, but there are some mountains. This photograph shows the Hombori cliffs, in Mali.

Kings Mansa Musa and Osei Tutu, and Queen Ndate Yalla Mbodj reigned during three important eras in West Africa. The stories of their lives help us to understand this region's history.

A map from 1375 shows King Mansa Musa enthroned in the kingdom of Mali.

Chapter Three

Mansa Musa, Emperor of Mali

It was the beginning of the year 1324. Mansa Musa, the emperor of Mali, had finished his fifth prayer of the day and was sitting, cross-legged, on his sheepskin mat. Musa was a pleasant-looking man. Dressed in a wide tunic worn over full pants and a shirt, his head wrapped in a white turban, the monarch was barefoot on his mat, as required by Muslim

Islam in West Africa

The religion, Islam, was revealed to the Arabian trader Muhammad in the seventh century. Islam began to expand south of the Sahara Desert in the eleventh century. It was introduced by **Berber** and Arab traders and was spread by black African traders and rulers. Islam shared a number of customs with traditional African religions, such as circumcision, communal prayers, and the ritual sacrifice of animals. The religion asked its followers to have faith in the one god, Allah, and to acknowledge Muhammad as his prophet; to pray five times a day; to give alms to the poor; to fast during **Ramadan,** and to make a pilgrimage to Mecca, the birthplace of Muhammad.

These children at a sidewalk school are studying the Koran, the sacred book of Islam.

tradition when one is praying. For the past hour, he had been reflecting.

Allah, his god, had been good to him. Mansa Musa was blessed with good health, his empire had grown, and his people had peace. At about forty years of age, he wanted to honor an important requirement of his religion—to make the *hajj*, the pilgrimage to Mecca in Arabia. He was a devout Muslim. The visit to the holy city of Islam is required of every believer who can afford the cost and is physically able to do it.

Mansa Musa was ready to travel, by horse, the 5,000 miles (8,000 km) of savanna and desert that lay between his capital of Niani and Mecca. He could get enough gold to pay the expenses of the long trip, but was the moment right? He would be absent for a year. Was his power solid enough? Were the borders of his empire secure enough so that he could leave his people and his land for such a long time?

He had been the *mansa*, or king, of Mali for sixteen years, and he had come far. In 1307, as a nephew of Sundiata, the founder of the Mali dynasty, he had inherited a weak empire. His first task had been to gain the loyalty of the governors and kings who headed the twelve regions and numerous kingdoms of his immense empire. Each governor ruled with the help of local leaders and traditional chiefs. These chiefs knew what the population needed, and they could tell the governors. The governors, in turn, reported to the mansa. Security was ensured by an army of about 100,000 men, stationed in garrisons all over the empire. Travelers were safe, and traders could go from one end of the empire to the other without fear of being robbed.

An ancient Mali sculpture shows that horses were used for travel.

15

Muslim prayer beads are made of 33, 66, or 100 beads. Believers use them to count the number of times they say the name of God or pray to God with particular formulas.

As he pulled his prayer beads, Mansa Musa felt reassured. His empire was strong. He trusted his governors and his generals to maintain peace and prosperity. His decision was made. He would go to Mecca. In his absence, his son, Maghan, would govern.

Preparing for the Hajj

Mansa Musa instructed the people of his court to prepare for the expedition. Every day, couriers left Niani on horseback to carry messages, written in Arabic by the emperor's secretaries, to his governors. Each province was asked for contributions of precious metals, crafts, and food.

Mali, the Mandingo Empire, had many copper and gold mines, and was the largest producer of gold in the world. Its goldsmiths created ornaments, weapons, and golden staffs for the dignitaries. The elegant women, draped in indigo cotton fabrics and silk brought by traders from Asia, wore delicate gold earrings, bracelets, and necklaces. The blacksmiths worked the copper and the iron to make tools, household utensils, and weapons. Farmers grew rice, millet (a grain), vegetables, and cotton on lands that were then fertile but have become arid over the centuries. In the rich pastures of the Senegal and Niger Valleys, herders raised cattle, goats, and sheep. The skins of the animals were tanned and dyed by craftsworkers who made delicate women's shoes, brightly colored boots and saddles for the horsemen, and large bags for the traders. Farmers, cattlemen, and craftsworkers all participated in the preparations for the great pilgrimage.

The emperor knew his journey would be long and difficult. Earlier rulers had made the hajj before him. Mansa Uli, the son of Sundiata Keita, had gone to Mecca in the 1260s. He was the first monarch to show the importance of the Mali Empire to the rulers of Egypt and Arabia. Sakura, a former slave and a general in Sundiata's army, became emperor at the end of the thirteenth century and then made the hajj. Unfortunately, he was killed by nomads on his way home. At his death, Mansa Musa assumed power.

*A **Fulani** woman of West Africa wears traditional jewelry. Gold was the greatest wealth of the Empire of Mali.*

The emperor's caravan was well armed and large enough to discourage any band of thieves. It is said that when the head of the caravan reached the city of Timbuktu, Mansa Musa was still in his palace in Niani, hundreds of miles away. According to accounts by Arab and local writers, 10,000 soldiers, 60,000 porters, 500 servants, and thousands of lawyers, doctors,

An old engraving shows a desert pilgrimage "of the grand caravan from Cairo to Mecca."

teachers, relatives, friends, and craftsworkers took part in the expedition. They followed Mansa Musa and his wife, Inari, on their way to becoming *El hajj* and *Adjaratu*, the titles given to Muslim men and women who have made the pilgrimage to the holy places of Islam.

Mansa Musa Reaches Egypt

After many weeks, the long convoy reached Egypt and camped near the pyramids outside Cairo. To announce his arrival, the emperor sent 50,000 **dinars** to the **sultan** of Egypt. The sultan, El Malick en Nasir, responded by offering the company the use of one of his palaces.

18

In July 1324, Mansa Musa entered Cairo, magnificently dressed, mounted on a horse, and surrounded by thousands of his subjects. He carried splendid presents created by his artisans and had much gold to give away. He and his company remained in the city for four months. He met with the sultan, dignitaries, the governor of Cairo, and learned people, and took pleasure in telling them about his country.

The Wealth of Mali

In the fourteenth century, the Empire of Mali spread over 1,000 miles (1,609 km), an area almost as vast as the United States east of the Mississippi. The capital, Niani, was on the Niger River and had at least 100,000 inhabitants. Hundreds of thousands of people lived in the 400 other cities, including Timbuktu, Jenne, and Gao, and the thousands of villages of the empire.

Mansa Musa had united many populations to form his empire. There were Mandingo farmers and traders scattered all over the land; Fulani, who moved

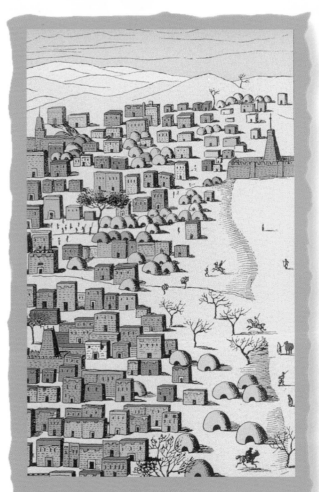

Long Way to Timbuktu

An old drawing shows the city of Timbuktu, which was founded in 1100. *Tim* means "the place of," and *Buktu* is a woman's name. Its university, Sankore, was renowned throughout the Muslim world. Europeans heard of the city's riches and tried to reach it, but did not succeed until 1828. Today, Timbuktu is a city of 35,000 people, with beautiful mosques and buildings protected as U.N. World Heritage Sites.

The Tuaregs are a fiercely independent people of the desert regions of West Africa.

Tuareg camel caravans carried salt across the Sahara.

from place to place with their cattle; **Tuareg** and Berber nomads of the sands of the Sahara; **Wolof** farmers and fishermen who lived along the Atlantic Coast; and Soninke farmers settled along the Senegal River. Some practiced traditional religions with many gods. Others had adopted Islam at the beginning of the eleventh century.

Travelers were impressed by the empire's wealth and noted that the people lived in comfort. Agriculture was well developed, and food was abundant. Traders led donkey and camel caravans across the empire, linking the lands of the North to those of the South. They bought goods in one place and sold them hundreds of miles away, exchanging salt and fabrics for ivory and gold.

Mansa Musa was proud of his empire and his people, and he wanted them to be known and remembered. One way to achieve that, he thought, was to display the great wealth of his land. He set out on his pilgrimage with two tons of gold that he used to buy supplies and to give away to people along his route. By the time he left Cairo, there was so much gold in circulation there that it was no longer rare and precious, and therefore its value dropped 25 percent.

Mansa Musa's visit made such an impression that two centuries later an Egyptian historian described it as the most remarkable event of 1324. Tales of the emperor's gold spread as far as Europe. A 1339 map drawn in Italy shows his empire, with the words *Rex Melli* (King of Mali). A 1375 map displays him holding a golden nugget, with the title *Musa Melli*.

A Wolof merchant of Senegal, in a drawing from 1854

Pilgrims circle the grand mosque in Mecca, Saudi Arabia, during a pilgrimage.

The Caravan Reaches Mecca

In October 1324, the ruler and his followers left Egypt for Arabia with a caravan of Egyptian pilgrims. In Mecca, Mansa Musa exchanged his rich clothes for two pieces of white cotton cloth, one draped around the body and one over the shoulders. Along with tens of thousands of other pilgrims, all dressed the same way as a sign of humility, equality, and fellowship, he performed the rites of the pilgrimage.

When Mansa Musa passed through Cairo again in February 1325, on his way back to Mali, he was impressed by the design of the Egyptian **mosques.** He asked a well-known architect, Es Saheli, to join his court. Es Saheli was a Muslim from Spain, a country that had been partly conquered by the Muslim Moors of North Africa in the eighth century.

The Emperor Returns to Mali

The emperor and his caravan returned to Niani in splendor. He immediately set his new architect to work building palaces in the cities of Gao and Niani. In the capital, Es Saheli planned an audience chamber for the emperor. It was a square room topped by a cupola and decorated with colorful designs called arabesques. He also built mosques in Gao, Jenne, and Timbuktu. Made of beaten earth reinforced by wood, the mosques were large, impressive buildings, well suited to the climate. They remained cool even when the temperature reached 110 degrees Fahrenheit (43 degrees Celsius). This was the traditional architecture in Mali, but it was refined and spread through the whole region. It can still be seen today in cities and towns from Senegal to Niger.

The emperor's mark was also felt on education. Like most Muslims, Mansa Musa read and wrote in Arabic. He encour-

Arabesques

These graceful designs of intertwined letters and floral and geometrical figures were created by the Arabs. The Italians called them *arabesco*, meaning "in the Arab manner," and that word became "arabesque."

A mosque made of beaten earth, along the Niger River in Mali

23

A book in Arabic, decorated in the "Arab manner," with floral designs and geometric figures

aged native scholars to write legal papers, religious literature, and poetry in Arabic, the language of Islam. He opened many schools for boys and girls, where they learned to read and write in Arabic and to recite the holy book of the Muslims, the Koran. He sent scholars to study in Morocco, a country then famous for its schools and universities.

Mansa Musa had established cultural and economic relations with the countries through which he traveled. He exchanged gifts and ambassadors with their rulers and with the merchant cities of North Africa.

During Mansa Musa's reign, the empire of Mali reached its height. It was peaceful, prosperous, and united. The ruler, an educated and religious man, stirred a cultural movement that transformed Jenne and Timbuktu into centers of learning.

These two cities had large libraries and thousands of schools that attracted scholars and students from West Africa, the **Maghreb**, and the Middle East.

While in Mecca, Mansa Musa had vowed to give up his throne and devote his life to prayer and learning. But when he returned to Niani, he saw that this was only a dream. His son, Maghan, was weak and lacked self-discipline. To pass on power to him would not be good for the empire.

However, when Mansa Musa died in 1337, Maghan succeeded him. As his father had feared, Maghan was a poor governor. After four years, he was overthrown by his uncle Suleyman, Mansa Musa's young brother. Mansa Suleyman had been close to Mansa Musa and continued his work.

Mansa Suleyman

"On his head is a turban which has fringes, they have a superb way of tying a turban. He is girt with a sword whose sheath is of gold, on his feet are boots and spurs. . . . In his hands there are two small spears, one of gold and one of silver with points of iron."—Ibn Battuta, Moroccan traveler and writer, 1352

The weekly market in Jenne, a city in Mali, with the town mosque in the background

An Asante "speaker," dressed in a kente cloth, holds the staff of office used since the sixteenth century. The gold-covered carving at the top illustrates a proverb, an important part of Asante culture.

Chapter Four

Osei Tutu, King of Asante

Manu Kototsii, the royal princess of Asante, had wished for a child for years but had not conceived. She consulted doctors and priests, yet no one in her small kingdom in the heart of present-day Ghana had been able to help. She decided to travel south with her husband to consult a group of priests in the kingdom of Nyanaw. Its king, Ansa Sasraku I,

Ghana and Ghana

The country called the Gold Coast by the Europeans took the name *Ghana* when it gained independence in 1957. It was never part of the empire of Ghana, which spread over parts of Senegal, Mali, and Mauritania.

called upon various priests to try to help the princess. Finally, while under the care of the priest of the **fetish** Otutu, she gave birth to a son.

The child was born on a Friday in or about 1660, and so was named Kofi. Asante people had seven names for boys and seven names for girls, one for each day of the week. When a child was born, he or she received the name reserved for that day. Boys born on a Friday were named Kofi, while girls born on that day were called Afua. Kofi was also given the name Tutu, for the fetish that had cured his mother. King Sasraku was generous, and the family remained with him until Kofi Tutu was about five years old. They then returned to Asante.

The Young Man Kofi

When Kofi reached adolescence, he was sent to the court of Boa Amponsem, in the kingdom of Denkyira, south of Asante. It was the custom for royal families of smaller kingdoms to send their sons to Denkyira as hostages. There they were educated and pledged their loyalty to the most powerful king of the region. In Denkyira, Kofi learned court manners, civil laws, and the traditions of the kingdom.

Things did not go as planned, though. The young

An 1846 illustration shows natives of the Gold Coast (Ghana) practicing their traditional religion.

28

man was soon in trouble for seducing Abena, the king's sister. She was married, and there was a great scandal. The king, his family, and the elders banished the young man. When he returned to Kwaman, the Asante capital, he found that the elders of his family were even angrier. They told him to leave the town. Kofi took refuge in Nyanaw with his godfather, Ansa Sasraku I. He remained with him for several years.

Time passed, and Kofi became a handsome man and a great dancer. He liked to have fun, and he was extravagant. He became a trader and bought and sold gold and other goods, traveling all over the kingdom of Sasraku I.

An important ceremonial object among the people of West Africa was the soul washer's disk, worn by rulers and members of the court, to protect them from danger.

Kofi was also interested in magic and fortune-telling. He befriended a priest, Okomfo Anokye, who traveled around the land, foretelling the future, curing the sick, and performing magic. The two began a friendship that would last a lifetime. From the first, Okomfo Anokye predicted that Tutu would fight many battles and become a great king.

In Kwaman, the royal family had problems. The king, Obiri Yeboa, Kofi's uncle, died in 1677, and a **regent** was appointed because the two sides of the family could not agree on a successor. After some years the family reconciled and turned to the next in line after the late Obiri Yeboa. The tradition in many African societies is that a ruler is succeeded

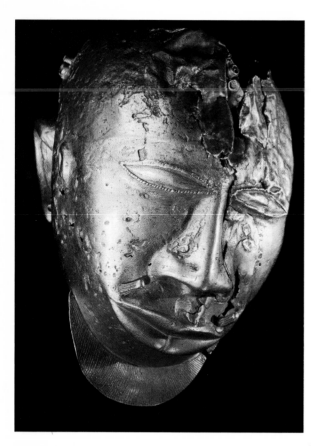

This gold portrait head may represent an important enemy ruler slain by the Asante.

not by a son but by a sister's son or daughter. So the heir to the Stool, as the Asante called the throne, would be the irresponsible Kofi Tutu.

Kofi was now in his twenties. He left Nyanaw accompanied by 500 subjects of King Sasraku. The young man who had fled Kwaman in shame returned as king. He was given the title reserved for a chief: Nana Osei Tutu.

Kofi Becomes Chief

Osei Tutu found his small nation disorganized and weak, so he set out to unify it. First, he reorganized the army. He established military service as an obligation for young men and imposed severe discipline. Those judged cowards were put to death. Those who made mistakes were fined or ridiculed. This last punishment was worse for the proud Asante than any other.

The 60,000-man army was divided into companies that marched into war in cross formation: a central column and two flanking wings. The Asante warriors used spears, swords, bows, and arrows. They wore protective helmets made of hard crocodile skin. Besides the traditional weapons of all Asante soldiers, elite fighters had rifles bought from traders who had settled on the Atlantic Coast south of Asante.

With a strong army, Osei Tutu went to war. His ambition was to make Asante powerful, and he set out to subdue his neighbors. He sold captured prisoners to Europeans for more weapons. He then forced the conquered kings into a confederation with Asante.

Osei Tutu controlled his allies by force, but he wanted to earn the loyalty of his new subjects in a peaceful way. With the help of the priest Okomfo Anokye, he devised a plan.

One day, all the chiefs and elders were summoned by the talking drums to a ceremony in the king's courtyard. Draped in a magnificent kente cloth, Tutu sat on his stool, surrounded by his mother, the stool-keepers, a line of soldiers, and a group of musicians. His neck, fingers, arms, and ankles were covered by huge gold ornaments. In the center of the yard, the priest

A great variety of designs and colors are used in kente cloth; some honor rulers or their families; others portray themes, such as peace or wealth.

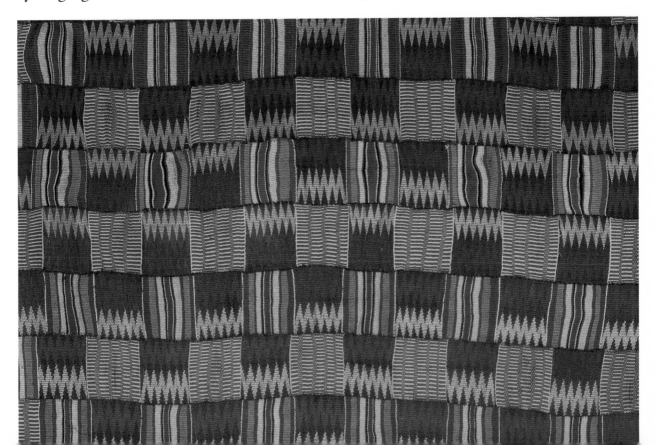

Talking With Drums

In parts of Africa, drums carry messages across long distances. A specific drumbeat is played as a signal for an occasion, and everyone knows what the beat means. A beat may call the people to a meeting or announce a visitor to the village. A series of beats that imitate the language may carry a longer message. Here, Asante drummers perform at a political rally in Ghana.

Anokye started to dance. As all eyes were on him, he suddenly produced a golden stool. Legends say that the stool descended from the skies. The priest presented the sacred object to Osei Tutu, telling the crowd that in it lay the unity, the soul, the wealth, and the power of the Asante nation. The Golden Stool became the symbol of Asante, a respected and unifying object, similar to the flags of modern nations.

A New Capital

Kwaman, the capital of Asante, was not grand enough to be the center of the great power that Asante had become, so Osei Tutu decided to found a new capital. He chose a site, and following an ancient tradition, the priest Okomfo Anokye planted a **kuma** tree there to represent the power of the ruler. As the tree grew, the priest predicted, Osei Tutu's power would expand. The capital was called Kumasi, which means "under the kuma tree."

The Asante king Otumfuo Opoku War II sits next to the Golden Stool, the symbol of the Asante nation.

Shameful Trade

Portugal, France, Great Britain, The Netherlands, Denmark, Sweden, and Prussia all set up trading posts, forts, and castles in the Gold Coast to oversee the trade in gold and, above all, slaves.

Kumasi was located at the meeting of two important roads, one leading north, the other south. From the north came Mandingo traders who exchanged metal goods, salt, fabrics, and leather for the Asante's kola nuts, ivory, and gold. In fact, there was so much gold in this region that Europeans called it the Gold Coast.

Through the Muslim traders, the kingdom was linked to the merchant cities of Timbuktu and Jenne, and beyond, to the cities of Tripoli in Libya, and Cairo in Egypt. To the south, the road led to the Atlantic Coast where the Europeans, who first came to Africa in 1444, had a flourishing business center. They traded firearms, ammunition, and other European goods for prisoners of war. In Europe, war captives were often killed. Africans thought it was kinder to make them slaves. From the middle of the fifteenth century, the Europeans began to buy some of the prisoners and ship them to the Americas.

Kumasi was the capital of the Asante kingdom in the seventeenth and eighteenth centuries.

Ancient Trade Routes

During the Middle Ages, Africa was a crossroads of trade. The region known as Sahel—south of the Sahara and north of the African forests, extending from Senegal to the Sudan—was one of the main commercial areas.

From the north, caravans of thousands of camels crossed the desert, led by Tuareg, Berber, and Arab traders. They carried salt, books, paper, silk, rugs, and other goods they had acquired in the rest of the Islamic world.

The Sahelian kingdoms and empires exported leather, ivory, pepper, gum arabic, gold, ostrich feathers, cotton, and cereals to the North. From the regions of Ghana and the Ivory Coast came gold, kola nuts, and ivory. East Africa traded with India and the Middle East through the Indian Ocean. Cowrie shells, used as money, were imported from the Maldive Islands off the coast of India.

The precious objects of Ghana shown here include a gold-dust spoon, a box for gold dust, weights, and cowrie shells.

From his new capital of Kumasi, Osei Tutu hoped to trade with the Europeans. He needed more firearms and ammunition to expand his empire. There was one obstacle to his plan:

the powerful kingdom of Denkyira. Its rulers demanded tribute from Asante and also blocked access to the coast. War seemed inevitable.

The king of Denkyira was Ntim Gyakari, and elders said he was Osei Tutu's son by the Princess Abena. Osei Tutu had seduced her as a youth. Gyakari had alliances with other clans and smaller kingdoms. He had an army of 100,000 men with three cannons he had bought from the Dutch. Osei Tutu's army had 60,000 men. After a year-long war, the Asante, although outnumbered, were victorious. King Ntim Gyakari was killed in a battle in 1701, and the kingdom of Denkyira was divided among Osei Tutu and his allies.

An eighteenth-century Asante weight for measuring gold showed two crocodiles with a shared stomach. Weights were a symbol of the state's wealth and power.

Osei Tutu Creates a State

Asante was now the most powerful state of the Gold Coast. To better govern, the king created a constitution. At the head of the nation was the king, called the *asantehene*. Each state of the federation was governed by its own leader, the *abrempon*. All the abrempons formed a council to advise the king in foreign affairs, such as declarations of war. Osei Tutu also created another council, the Asante *kotoko*. Kotoko means "porcupine" and like that small animal, the council, if attacked, could inflict much harm. The queen mother, some chiefs, and the principal elders were all part of the council.

To unify his kingdom, Osei Tutu introduced an annual *Odwira* festival. The celebration honored the nation's dead kings and ancestors. All participants, including the chiefs, renewed their vows to the king.

Osei Tutu's main interest was to expand and strengthen his state. However, he also cared about his people's needs. To improve his land and his subjects' lives, he began important public works. The swamps surrounding Kumasi were breeding grounds for mosquitoes and other insects, so he had them drained and turned into cultivated plots. Canals were built along the River Suben to improve navigation, and commerce with African and European merchants was increased.

Osei Tutu also continued his wars of expansion. He was generally successful, but the kingdom of Akyem, in the

Odwira

The Odwira purification festival is held over a period of forty days, with many rituals and events, including invocations of spirits and the blessing of ceremonial swords.

At Asante traditional festivals, the king's regalia—including this European-style chair—is carried in procession by members of the court.

Today, Kumasi is an important city in Ghana. Colorful buildings are common in Kumasi.

southeast, refused to submit. Its king refused to pay the tribute demanded by the asantehene. In 1717, war broke out between the mighty Asante confederation and Akyem.

A Lost Battle

Osei Tutu was in his fifties and sick, but he wanted to direct an important battle. His warriors carried him in a hammock to the battle scene where the army was pursuing the retreating Akyem. But the Akyem were not in flight—they were moving back to lure on the Asante. When the Asante army started to cross the River Prah, the Akyem attacked and killed the king. The Asante army retreated to Kumasi after this terrible defeat.

Three years of disorder followed Osei Tutu's death. Finally his nephew, Opoku Ware, succeeded him and was able to bind the confederation together and further expand the territory—even conquering Akyem.

Osei Tutu, the once-immature and mischievous prince, had become the most important king of Asante. Under his leadership, his nation grew in less than twenty years from a small kingdom to the largest, richest, and most powerful state of the Gold Coast.

The country is now called Ghana. Although it is governed by an elected president, the traditional leaders of Asante still use the Golden Stool, follow the constitution, and gather their people for the Odwira festival.

The skilled gold workers of the Asante kingdom produced these finely worked items: a crown, band, sandals, a sculpture for the top of a staff, and a sword with gold-leaf trimming.

Men play the traditional instrument, the kora, made from a gourd at a festival to celebrate Senegal's independence from France in 1960.

Chapter Five

Ndate Yalla Mbodj, Queen of Walo

In September 1846, Queen Njombot Mbodj, who had reigned for sixteen years over Walo, a Wolof kingdom in northern Senegal, died. She was the highest-ranking female in the royal family, and fifteen years earlier she had influenced the kingdom's council in the choice of the *brak*, or king. The king, Fara Penda, was weak, and Njombot had assumed power, although she was not the official ruler. When Penda died, she again influenced the choice of the brak and another weak king, Malik Mbodj, was chosen. Njombot, as she had planned from the beginning, remained the only decision maker. Now that she was dead, the council did not want the king to govern. Njombot's son, Prince Ely, was only twelve and too young to rule. The next in line was the queen's younger sister, Ndate Yalla Mbodj, and she became the queen mother, or *linguer*, of Walo.

A nineteenth-century drawing shows a young Wolof girl.

Linguer of Walo

Ndate Yalla was a good-looking woman. Although the queen, she dressed modestly, like her subjects. She lived in the capital, Nder, in a vast palace with rooms separated by large courtyards patrolled by soldiers. When Ndate Yalla gave an audience, 500 women who formed her court surrounded her. Her husband, Tasse, did not sit with her. He remained with the princes on the opposite side of the courtyard.

What's in a Name?

In Walo, the custom was to give princesses names that carried a hopeful message. *Njombot* means "burgeon"—to grow or flourish—and it was hoped that a child given this name would bloom into an important woman. *Ndate Yalla* means "graces of God," which may have been an effort to attract God's benevolence.

Ndate Yalla, the Queen of Walo (left), and her husband (right), the King of Walo

The royal families who had governed Walo since its foundation in the thirteenth century were not wealthy. The country was fertile but lacked gold and minerals. Most of the people were farmers who grew millet and vegetables along the banks of the Senegal River. Nomads tended cattle in pastures deep in the heart of the land. The Atlantic Ocean and the rivers teemed with fish, and every day fishermen hauled in thousands of pounds with their nets. Craftsworkers, hunters, and traders provided other necessities. The people produced enough for their own needs. There were no big cities, and

A pirogue *(traditional dugout canoe) on the Senegal River*

most of the population lived in villages or in a few larger towns with only about 5,000 inhabitants.

From time to time, neighboring people had invaded Walo. So, the rulers maintained an army of about 10,000, including 4,000 horsemen, to defend the territory.

When Ndate became linguer, her small kingdom had been in a difficult situation for a long time. Located at the mouth of the Senegal River, Walo was coveted by the Moors who lived on the northern side of the river. The Moors were fierce nomads who had invaded the kingdom many times. To the west, the French who had arrived in the sixteenth century had built the city of Saint-Louis in 1659 and used it as a trading post. They exchanged European goods for gold, ivory, hides, gum arabic, and—above all—slaves. Many of the enslaved men were prisoners of war, but the women and children were often

Gum Arabic

These acacia trees of Senegal produce a gum used to make chewing gum and glue. Gum was introduced to Europe by the Arabs and was therefore called Gum Arabic.

victims of kidnapping. The hunt for men, women, and children was so devastating that in 1673, the population of Walo, led by a Muslim priest, revolted against the slave trade. The people overthrew the king who had helped the French in their slave-dealing activities.

Finally, France, with the help of some neighboring rulers, crushed the Walo revolt, burned the villages and seized thousands of men, women, and children, and shipped them to America as slaves.

In 1848, two years after Ndate Yalla became queen, France abolished slavery. Although the French were no longer looking for slaves, they still wanted to control Walo.

The End of Independence

Now Ndate Yalla faced a difficult situation. Should she side with the Moors or with the French? They both wanted her

The Moors

The Moors from North Africa, a mix of Berber and Arab people, occupied parts of Spain, Portugal, and Italy between the eighth and fifteenth centuries. They built mosques and palaces, and they developed commercial, cultural, and intellectual societies. The Moors also occupied areas of Mali and Senegal. Today, the term refers only to an ethnic group in Mauritania.

land. Her kingdom was weak, and if she did not choose a powerful ally, it might be invaded and crushed by the other side.

The French in Saint-Louis wanted to conquer the river kingdom of Walo quickly, but the queen resisted. She put a

Tribute

To trade in the region, the French were made to pay tribute—annual fees or taxes—to the rulers of the various kingdoms.

tax on cattle led through her territory. When the governor in Saint-Louis protested, she wrote to him, "this country belongs to us and we must govern it; we guarantee the safe passing of the herds through our country, therefore we take one-tenth and we will never accept anything else. Saint-Louis belongs to the governor and Walo to the brak, each governs his country as he sees fit."

Angry, the French refused to pay tribute to Walo. But Ndate Yalla stood up to them. She denied them access to one area of her kingdom after another. Finally, she warned them that they had to leave her territory or there would be war.

On February 20, 1855, a French force marched on Walo, but was stopped by the Walo army and the population. A larger detachment was then sent out, but Ndate Yalla called up her army and asked the army of the Moors for support. After a six-month campaign, the French defeated Walo. They

The tax on African cattle led to war.

burned seventy villages, killed dozens of people, and took thousands of cattle and sheep. In December 1855, Walo became a French territory.

A scene from the French-Senegal war

Exile in Kayor

Ndate Yalla, with her husband, their son Sidia, and her nephew Ely, took refuge in Kayor. They placed themselves under the protection of the *damel* (king) of Kayor, and the *serin* (Muslim leader) of the holy town of Niomre.

From Kayor, the queen's army continued to harass the French troops for years. They were such a nuisance that France repeatedly asked their protectors to turn them over. The damel of Kayor and the serin of Niomre, however, refused.

47

A modern Wolof woman

In 1858, in a last effort to subdue Ndate Yalla, the French invaded Niomre. The Wolof queen was away at the time, but her son Sidia was there. The religious authorities refused to give him up, so the French ransacked the city.

Ndate Yalla and her family remained in exile for two more years, until they reached an agreement with France. They were allowed to return to their former kingdom, which was then ruled by a French governor, in exchange for a promise not to fight the French. Ndate Yalla had no more power. She accepted the treaty because she hoped that her son Sidia could someday win back the throne.

Ndate Yalla soon died, but Sidia continued in his mother's path. In 1869, he led a revolt of the population of Walo against the French. He allied himself with the new damel of Kayor, Lat Dior Diop, with whom, years earlier, he had harassed the French army. They, too, were defeated and Sidia was sent to Gabon, in Central Africa.

Ndate Yalla was the last linguer of Walo. She fiercely resisted French rule and her defeat marked the end of an era in Africa. Walo was the first kingdom south of the Sahara to be conquered by France. Based in Walo, the French were able to defeat the other kingdoms until the whole country of Senegal became a French colony. The French then conquered fifteen countries in Africa south of the Sahara. In the 1960s, these territories regained their independence, 100 years after the death of the queen who was among the first to resist the European conquest, linguer Ndate Yalla Mbodj.

This street is one of many in Dakar, the capital of Senegal. On June 19, 1960, Senegal declared its independence from France.

Chapter Six

West Africa Today

Yesterday's West Africa of powerful kingdoms and large empires has been divided
into sixteen countries. After seventy-five
years of colonization, nearly all these
nations gained their independence in the
1960s. Ghana had become independent in
1957, and the former Portuguese colonies
fought to gain their freedom in 1974.

Today's West Africa is very different
from the way it was in the times of Osei
Tutu and Ndate Yalla Mbodj, but it has
still retained many of its traditions. Its

Traditions and modern life complement each other. A gold-decked Asante chief and his daughter take part in a polictical rally in Ghana.

cities teem with millions of people and cars, and West Africa has all the modern conveniences that can be found in Europe and America. But at the same time, people continue to value their own way of life, their native dress, their languages, their customs, and their culture.

History is taught in schools, and musicians, storytellers, playwrights, filmmakers, painters, and writers keep stories of the past alive for eager audiences.

Far from being forgotten, the kings and queens who brought new ideas, developed the land, encouraged creativity, and passed on valuable innovations to future generations are still present in the lives and minds of today's West Africans.

A traditional griot, or storyteller, captivates his young audience. Storytellers often tell stories about famous kings and queens.

Glossary

Allah—the word *Allah* means "God" in Arabic

Berber—an inhabitant of North Africa. Berbers preceded the Arabs, who came from Arabia in the seventh century.

dinar—Egyptian money

fetish—an object believed to have special powers

Fulani—a large and widespread African people. *Fulani* is the plural of the name, and the singular is *Pulo.*

Islam—a religion based on a belief in one god—Allah—and in Muhammad as his prophet

kente cloth—bright, handwoven cotton fabric with geometric designs, made by the Asante people

kuma—a sacred tree in Kumasi

Maghreb—the area formed by the North African countries of Morocco, Algeria, Tunisia, and Libya.

mosque—a building for Islamic prayers, teaching, and worship

Muhammad—in the faith of Islam, the prophet to whom Allah revealed his religion

Muslim—a follower of Islam

Ramadan—in Islam, a thirty-day period of fasting observed each year, to build self-discipline, to understand the hard lot of the poor, and to appreciate the compassion of God who gives people what they need to live

regent—a person who rules in place of a monarch

sultan—an Arabic word meaning the king or ruler of a Muslim people

Tuareg—a nomadic people living in the Sahara

Wolof—a people living in Senegal and Gambia

To Find Out More

Books

Binns, Tony. *West Africa*. Austin, TX: Raintree Steck-Vaughn, 1998.

Blauer, Ettagale, and Jason Lauré. *Ghana*. Danbury, CT: Children's Press, 1999.

Bleeker, Sonia. *The Ashanti of Ghana*. New York: Morrow, 1996.

Brooks, Larry. *Daily Life in Ancient and Modern Timbuktu*. Minneapolis, MN: Runestone, 1999.

Harris, Colin. *A Taste of West Africa*. New York: Thomson Learning, 1995.

McKissack, Patricia. *The Royal Kingdoms of Ghana, Mali, and Songhay: Life in Medieval Africa.* New York: Holt, 1994.

Millar, Heather. *The Kingdom of Benin in West Africa.* Tarrytown, NY: Benchmark Books, 1997.

Minks, Louise. *Traditional Africa.* San Diego: Lucent Books, 1996.

Myers, Walter Dean. *At Her Majesty's Request: An African Princess in Victorian England.* New York: Scholastic Press, 1999.

Nwanunobi, C. Onyeka. *The Malinke.* New York: Rosen Publishing Group, 1996.

Roundtree, Katherine. *My Little African King.* Inglewood, CA: Black Butterfly, 2000.

Sallah, Tijan M. *The Wolof.* New York: Rosen Publishing Group, 1996.

Thompson, Carol. *The Asante Kingdom.* Danbury, CT: Franklin Watts, 1999.

———. *The Empire of Mali.* Danbury, CT: Franklin Watts, 1999.

Organizations and Online Sites

Africa: The Art of a Continent: Western Africa
http://artnetweb.com/guggenheim/africa/west.html
Go to this nested page within the Guggenheim Museum site to learn more about the art of West Africa.

African Art Museum of Maryland
5430 Vantage Point Road
Columbia, MD 21044
See the art and cultural objects of Africa in this museum.

Ashanti
http://www.ashanti.com.au
If you want to learn more about the history of the Asante Kingdom, including its rulers, family system, and art, go to this site.

Ghana Web
http://ghanaweb.com/
This extensive site includes information on business, culture, government, education, religion, and much more.

Homowo Foundation for African Arts and Culture
2915 NE 15th Avenue
Portland, OR 97202
This organization promotes African culture through the performing arts.

Kings of Africa
http://www.tamarin.com/kings/kindire1.htm
See many photographs of African kings at this site.

The National Museum of African Art
950 Independence Avenue, SW
Washington, D.C. 20560
http://www.si.edu/nmafa/
Part of the Smithsonian Institution, this museum promotes understanding of the diverse cultures in Africa through the visual arts.

San Francisco African American Historical and
Cultural Society
Ft. Mason Center – Building C
762 Fulton Street
San Francisco, CA 94123
The society presents educational programs on the history and culture of African and African-American people.

West Africa
http://www.westafrica.com
Visit this site to learn about the art, culture, history, and industry of West Africa.

A Note on Sources

I used a variety of sources to write *Kings and Queens of West Africa*. Some were translations of books written in Arabic by fourteenth-century North African travelers and by fifteenth-century black Africans. Other books were written in French, the official language of Mali and Senegal.

I consulted, in particular: *General History of Africa* (eight volumes), published by UNESCO and the University of California Press; *Ibn Battuta in Black Africa* by Said Hamdun; *Historical Dictionary of Mali* by Pascal James Imperato; *Ancient Ghana and Mali* by Nehemia Levtzion; *Osei Tutu of Asant* by Kwame Yeboa Daaku; *Ashanti Heroes* by Kyeretwie Bansu; *Osei Tutu: The Leopard Owns the Land* by Basil Freestone; *Esquisses Sénégalaises* by Abbé David Boilat; *Le Royaume du Waalo* by Boubacar Barry; *Historical Dictionary of Senegal* by Andrew F. Clark.

—*Sylviane Anna Diouf*

Index

Numbers in *italics* indicate illustrations.

Abena (princess of
  Denkyira), 29, 36
Abrempon council, 36
Agriculture, 6, 9, 16, 19, 20,
  21, 37, 43
Akyem kingdom, 37–38, 39
Ansa Sasraku I (king of
  Nyanaw), 27–28, 29, 30
Arabic, 7, 16, 23, 24
Arabs, 14, 17, 35, 44, 45
Architecture, 22, 23, *23*
Arts, 6, *15*, *24*, *29*, *30*, *39*
Asante people, the, 10, 11,
  26, 27–39, *33*, *52*
  constitution, 36–37, 39

Bantu people, the, 7
Berber people, the, 14, 21,
  35
Boa Amponsem (king of
  Denkyira), 28, 29

Cairo, Egypt, 19, 21, 22, 34
Colonization, 6, 11, 49, 51
Crafts, 6, 16, 17, *17*, 18, *24*,
  29, 39, 43

Denkyira kingdom, 28, 36

Education, 6, 14, 18, 23–25,
  24, 28, 53, *53*
Egypt, 10, 17, 18–19, 22,
  34
El Malick en Nasir (sultan of
  Egypt), 18
Ely (prince of Walo), 42, 47
Es Saheli, 22
Europeans, 6, 7, 10–11, 28,
  31, 34, 35, 49. *See also*
  specific countries

Fara Penda (king of Walo),
  41–42

French, 11, 34, 44–47, *47*, 49

French-Senegal War, 46–47, *47*

Fulani people, the, *17*, 19–20

Gabon, 49

Gao, Mali, 19, 23

Ghana, *6*, 11, 27, 28, *28*, *32*, 39, 51, *52*
  ancient, 10, 28, 35

Gold, 11, 15, 16, 21, 29, 34, 35, 36, *39*, 42, 44

Gold Coast, 11, 28, *28*, 34, 36, 39

Golden Stool, the, *32*, 39

Hajj, 14–22, *18*, *22*

Ibn Battuta, 25

Inari, 18

Islam, 10, 13–15, *14*, 16, *16*, 17, 18, 22, 23–25, *23*, 25, 34, 45

Ivory, 21, 35, 44

Jenne, Mali, 19, 23, 24–25, *25*, 34

Kayor, 47

Kente cloth, *26*, 31, *31*

Kotoko council, 36–37

Kumasi, 33–34, *34*, 35, 37, 38, *38*

Kwaman, 29, 30, 33

Lat Dior Diop (king of Kayor), 47, 49

Maghan (king of Mali), 16, 25

Maghreb, the, 25

Maldive Islands, 35

Mali, 10, *11*, *12*, 13, 28, 45

Malik Mbodj (king of Walo), 42

Mandingo people, the, 19, 34

Mansa Musa (king of Mali), 10, 11, *12*, 13–25

Mansa Suleyman (king of Mali), 25

Mansa Uli (king of Mali), 17

Manu Kototsii (princess of the Asante), 27, 31

Mauritania, 28, 45

Mecca, Saudi Arabia, 13, 15, 16, 22, *22*, 25

Moors, 22, 44, 45, *45*, 46

Morocco, 10, 24

Ndate Yalla Mbodj (queen of
Walo), 10, 11, 41–49, *43*,
51
Nder, Walo, 42
Niani, Mali, 15, 16, 17, 19,
23, 25
Niomre, 47, 49
Njombot Mbodj (queen of
Walo), 41–42
North Africa, 7, 9, 22, 24, 45
Ntim Gyakari (king of
Denkyira), 36
Nyanaw kingdom, 27–28, 29,
30

Obiri Yeboa (king of the
Asante), 29
Odwira festival, 37, *37*, 39
Okomfo Anokye, 29, 31–32,
33
Opoku Ware (king of the
Asante), 38–39
Osei Tutu (king of the
Asante), 10, 11, 27–39,
51

Portuguese, 11, 34, 51

Religions, indigenous, 27–28,

28, 29, 29, 31–32, 33, 37,
37, 39
Sahel, the, 35
Saint-Louis, 44, 45, 46
Senegal, 10, 11, *20*, 28, 35,
40, 41, 45, 49
Sidia (prince of Walo), 47, 49
Slave trade, 6, 10–11, 31, 34,
44–45
Sudan, 35
Sundiata Keita (king of
Mali), 10, 15, 17

Tasse (king of Walo), 42, *43*,
47
Timbuktu, Mali, *8–9*, 17, 19,
19, 23, 24–25, 34
Trade, 6, 9, 10, 14, 15, 19,
20, 21, *25*, 29, 30, 34–36,
35, 37, 43, 44, 46, *46*
slave, 6, 10–11, 31, 34,
44–45
Tuareg people, the, *20*, 21,
35

Walo, 10, 11, 41–49, *44*
Wolof people, the, 21, *21*,
41–49, *42, 44, 48*

About the Author

Sylviane Anna Diouf is the author of fiction and nonfiction books for adults and children and of numerous articles for international publications. She specializes in the history of Africa and of people of African origin.

Of Senegalese and French parentage, Ms. Diouf has lived in various African and European countries and in the United States. She has traveled in many parts of the world and speaks several languages. She holds a doctorate from the University of Paris and lives in New York City with her son.

George Mason Library
2601 Cameron Mills Rd.
Alexandria, Virginia 22302